MW00748649

LOST in the RAIN FOREST

Cheryl Lynne Crouch

Beacon Hill Press of Kansas City
Kansas City, Missouri

ISBN 083-411-6480

Printed in the United States of America

Editor: Bruce Nuffer
Assistant Editor: Micah W. Moseley

Cover Design and Illustration: Ted Ferguson
Illustrations by: Dave Howard

Note: This book is part of the *Understanding Christian Mission,* Children's Mission Education curriculum. It is designed for use in Year 2, The Bible in Mission. This study year examines the importance of the Bible in the mission enterprise. This book was chosen for use in this year because it gives children insights into the importance of the Bible to missionaries themselves as well as to the unsaved. This book is based on the true story of Kosal and his village.

10   9   8   7   6   5   4   3   2   1

Our special thanks to Vern Ward
for telling us about Kosal and his village.
He shared a story that will long be
remembered by many who read it.

Chapter 1

"You think you're so tough?" Chad whispered fiercely. He realized the words would be more impressive if he looked tougher. So he scrunched up his face and tried to look mean. It wasn't easy. He was small and bony with big freckles and even bigger glasses.

"Yeah, I'm tough," his brother answered with a smirk. Andy, who was big and muscular, was intimidating even when he didn't mean to be.

Chad's heart raced. "You just wait and I'll . . . I'll . . . Ouch!" he grimaced as he felt a sharp pain on his arm. He knew it was his mom. She gave him one of those "You better be quiet and I mean it!" looks.

Chad rolled his eyes. Having his mother thump him didn't do much for his tough guy image. Chad did not like sitting with his parents. He wanted to sit with the other kids in the back of the church. That way he wouldn't be within range of Mom's flicking finger.

"Way to go, tough guy," Andy whispered, chuckling. Chad felt his face grow warm. How did Andy always get the last laugh?

Chad decided now would be a good time to pay attention to the missionary speaker. The man described a rope bridge that he crossed to get to a village. It was shaped like an upside-down triangle. It had one thick rope at the bottom to walk on. There was a rope on each side to grab with your hands. And there were shorter ropes running from the hand ropes to the bottom rope in the middle. The missionary said it was a bit like tightrope walking. Chad's imagination flew.

He imagined a rotting rope bridge. It swung violently in the midday wind. A river flowed a thousand feet below. The missionary walked carefully across. Chad's heart beat faster. He pictured the man—what was his name? Dr. Wally Anderson?

He pictured Dr. Anderson walking on an actual tightrope. There were no ropes for his hands. He steadied himself with outstretched arms. "Oh," Chad thought, "a waterfall would be even scarier!"

So Chad imagined the missionary carefully inching above rocky falls. But the falls were not just any falls. They were the Niagara Falls!

A large audience gathered to watch. Chad held his breath. The brave man slowly worked his way across. The winds blew harder. Water crashed in white foam below. The roar of the water was deafening. Dr. Anderson couldn't even hear the crowds cheering him on. Chad feared the missionary would not make it all the way across. Yet he kept up a steady advance across the rope. He was so close to the end Chad began to believe he might make it. Then tragedy struck.

With only eight feet to go, Dr. Anderson lost his balance. It happened in slow motion. Chad gasped as he watched the man fall to certain death. But wait! He caught the rope with his hands! Wally the Wonder Walker hung above the falls. The crowd sat in stunned silence. Would he have the strength to hold on?

Dr. Anderson swung his legs. His body looped around, and he sat on the rope. To Chad's amazement, he stood back up. He held his hands wide and smiled at the crowd. Then Dr. Wally almost ran the final steps to the platform.

"WOW!" Chad shouted and clapped wildly.

His mother yelped, "Chad!" Chad's daydream disappeared. He was back in the Gainesville First missionary service with a jolt. He'd done it again. He let his daydream get so real that he acted on it. Even worse, it happened at church.

"Sometimes I am so embarrassed for you!" Andy whispered before he put his head in his hands.

Chad felt his face grow warm again. But it did not last. To Chad's amazement, others in the church began to clap. It started slowly with a few people. Then the whole congregation applauded.

For a minute Chad thought maybe the others had actually seen Wally the Wonder Walker too. He did not realize his outburst occurred at the right moment. The missionary had just told about a revival in a village in Papua New Guinea (PAH-pwaw new GI-nee). At least 35 people had accepted Christ as their Savior.

Now, Chad's church was not a church to go applauding at just anything. In fact, Chad could only remember four times in his life that he had heard applause there. But because of his prompting, it happened again.

The missionary almost had a heart attack. He quit speaking and looked around in shock. A smile quickly swept across his face. The revival excited him. But the people in the churches didn't usually share his excitement. He belted out with a "Hallelujah!" Then he went on to give the best message he had ever given.

10

He said there are over 700 languages spoken in Papua New Guinea, and that trying to spread the gospel is very difficult. He told about how translators work year after year to make a Bible for each language group in the country.

Chad's parents forgot all about his slip. Their eyes focused on the missionary. After the service, the missionary went right over to Chad. He wanted to meet the boy who was so excited about missions. Chad's dad started talking before Dr. Anderson could ask Chad any questions. Chad was relieved. But the relief did not last long. Chad's dad asked if Papua New Guinea needed doctors. Chad almost fell over!

"Surely he's not thinking of himself," Chad thought. "He wouldn't just pick up and move us. We'd have to live in grass huts and learn 700 languages! Yikes!"

The missionary explained about something called Nazarenes in Voluntary Service. "With NIVS," said Dr. Anderson, "you pay your own way. It's a wonderful help to the missionaries. They have so many needs. And with the lack of Bibles, we always need more living witnesses of God's Word."

Chad decided to leave while Dr. Anderson talked to his dad. He was still a little embarrassed about his outburst. There was no place to hide in the sanctuary. He wanted to go home.

He found his mom in the church foyer. She was talking to a friend. He waited politely until they finished. "Mom, can I get your keys and walk home?"

"Yes, dear," she answered. "Your father and I will talk with you when we get there."

"Great," Chad thought. He took the keys and headed out the church door. His parents had talked to him before about his problem with daydreams. He had gotten into trouble a few times in school. And though he was very bright, his grades suffered. He had trouble staying focused on his lessons.

He continued down the road to his house. Halfway, he wondered what his punishment would be. Then he corrected "punishment" to "consequence." His dad always says that his actions have consequences. If Chad would control his actions, he might have fewer negative consequences. "But how do I control my imagination?" he wondered.

Even as he wondered, his overeager imagination kicked in. "What will be tonight's consequence? They will hook my brain to a machine. It will remove my imagination cells one cell at a time. Then they will store them in a computer, where . . .

"A computer!" Chad came back to reality fast. It was very likely his parents would ground him from his new computer. He'd had it for almost a week. He spent most of his free time using it. He could let his imagination run wild without getting into trouble.

Chad's shoulders drooped. Having his computer taken away not only was less glamorous than having his imagination cells removed but also would be much more painful.

He turned in at the driveway and approached his house. It was a beautiful two-story brick home with trees around it. Chad's mom loved the trees. Chad and Andy agreed that she loved them because she never had to mow around them. And she did not have to bag the hundreds of leaves in the fall. Disliking those tasks was one of the few agreements Chad and Andy had.

Chad went into his house and headed upstairs to

his room. He planned to use his computer until they dragged his body away from it.

He was in the middle of an intense game of Land of the Locomquots when he heard a knock on his bedroom door. He answered, "Come in, Dad." Chad turned off his beloved machine and braced himself.

If he had known what his dad was really going to say, Chad would have thought being grounded from the computer was nothing!

Chapter 2

In Papua New Guinea, inside a hut of bamboo and grass, lay a very sick man. His only comfort was a dried banana-leaf mat on the dirt floor. Talking filtered through the little room. Four men crouched by the fire. As it crackled and hissed, they whispered in the language of their people.

A short man wearing an old, dirty T-shirt and a loincloth was speaking. The leaves in his hair shook as he talked. "There is not another witch doctor to help us. All of those within a day's walk have come to work their magic on Kosal (KO-sil). But he keeps getting weaker. He won't live much longer. We must do something."

"Do something, yes," an older man answered in a quiet, raspy voice. He wore a dusty tweed sports coat, which was a symbol of his authority. The others listened to him with respect. "What can we do? We have tried the government health centers."

"Four of them," an angry young man asserted. He wore a dress shirt and jeans. He was the only one wearing shoes. "We carried him, on a cot, over the mountain to the north," he said. "We walked for a whole day, crossing 25 rivers. But after all that, they could do nothing for him."

The last member of the group spoke. He was Kosal's brother. His watery eyes stared at the floor. "Then two days to the south we carried him," he said.

"And then to the east and the west. But all of these clinics said they do not know what is wrong with Kosal. I am afraid the end is near. We have done all we can do."

"How can you give up?" asked the angry youth. "He is Kosal! He is our chief! This man has earned the title of chief because of his goodness." It was true. Among Kosal's people, the kindest and most giving person is elected chief. "He is generous and smart and has led us well," said the young man. "Why are you so eager to let him go?"

Kosal's brother turned his sad eyes on the youth. "Eager? Young man, you speak foolishly. Of course we do not want to let Kosal pass on to the spirit world. But what can we do?"

The two older men echoed, "What can we do?"

"I'll tell you what we can do. If you really want to save our chief, you will agree. We must send him to the hospital in Kudjip (KOO-jip)!"

"What makes you think this hospital in Kudjip can help him? What do you know about it?" asked the man with leaves in his hair.

The youth was anxious to share what he knew. "Last year I flew on the airplane. We went to sell the coffee beans we had. While I was in the city, I heard about this hospital. They have a God that they pray to when they give medicine. This God has the power to heal with the medicine. Some people, who can't get well anywhere else, get well there!" He spoke boldly. He was proud to know something his village elders didn't know. But he didn't expect them to send Kosal to the hospital. Their response surprised him.

"If these doctors and their God can help Kosal, we need to get him to Kudjip," Kosal's brother said.

The man with the leaves agreed. "We've tried everything else. It's our only hope."

The three men who had spoken turned to the old man. Even the young man respected this elder's opinion. They were silent as they waited for him to speak.

The flickering fire reflected in the old, dark eyes as he thought about the idea. "We need to do all we can for Kosal," he agreed.

"Exactly!" exclaimed the young man.

The old man's eyebrows shot up, creating a whole new set of wrinkles. He cleared his throat. "We need to do all we can, but I am worried about Kudjip. The spirits of that village must be very powerful."

He looked into the fire again. The young coffee trader bit his tongue. He wanted to say that that was exactly the point. Finally, the wrinkled mouth began to move again. "Maybe those spirits are more powerful than our own spirits. What if their spirits come back here? They might overcome our spirits and destroy us."

The others had not considered that. They were afraid of what Kudjip's spirits might do. They knew all about evil spirits, and they lived in fear of them. Finally the sad man said, "What do we do? Even if the hospital can help Kosal, should we risk the welfare of our whole village? How could we find out more about what might happen?"

This time the younger man was more hesitant. "I . . . I know a man from Kudjip village. He lives at Dusin (DEW-sin) now. That's not far from here. I could ask him to help us if you want me to." He looked down, waiting for someone to tell him to hold his tongue. Instead he heard a quiet, raspy voice say, "I think that is an excellent idea. Go speak to him tomorrow morning."

The men continued to look into the fire. They thought about the importance of the decisions they had to make. They did not look at Kosal. In his sickness, he had floated in and out of consciousness during the talk. They did not know that he had heard them. He agreed with their decision. If the men had looked at him, they would have seen his lips curve into a smile.

Chapter 3

Chad's bedroom door swung open slowly. He looked up at his dad. Dr. Wilson's tall, muscular body filled the doorway. His head almost touched the top of the doorframe as he stepped through it.

Chad felt a surge of pride. Everyone respected Dr. Wilson. Chad always liked being known as "Dr. Wilson's son." Maybe that made tonight worse. He wondered if it embarrassed his dad to be known as "Chad's father"?

Dr. Wilson's kind eyes looked at Chad's. Chad dropped his head in shame. Why had he embarrassed his dad—his whole family—the way he had tonight?

"Chad, we have some talking to do," his dad said at last. "Why don't you come on down to the family room?"

Chad jerked his head back up. "The family room?" he asked, surprised.

"Yes," his dad said. "We have something important to discuss. It involves the whole family."

Chad's thoughts whirled like a tornado inside his head. "The whole family! No, not Andy!"

Chad wondered if they were going to let Andy help determine his consequences. "Probably," he thought. "They don't know Andy's bad side. They only see him as Mr. Perfect Son."

"In fact," Chad thought, "probably no one besides me knows that Andy can be less than perfect."

Therefore, it would be to Andy's benefit to have Chad done away with. Andy would have him locked in that dark, smelly storage room for weeks. Andy knew Chad was afraid of the storage room.

Chad finally got his tongue to work. "That's not fair!" he cried out. But his dad had already left the room.

Chad took his time going down the stairs. He felt he was a prisoner heading for an unjust trial. In the hallway, he paused to say good-bye to Chuckles, his wiener dog. Chad shuffled on, letting his head hang heavily. His hands hung limply until he needed one to wipe a lonely tear puddling up inside his glasses. He removed the thick frames and wiped them on his shirt. With each step he felt sorrier for himself.

When he entered the room, Chad noticed Andy's smirk. This was going to be the worst!

"Chad, come sit down," Mrs. Wilson said sweetly. "We have a big decision to make."

"Yeah," Andy added gleefully. "What to do with my brainless brother so he won't keep embarrassing all of us! Obviously, we can't keep taking him out in public!"

Chad thought, "Oh, great. Here comes the storage room idea."

"Andy, hush," Mrs. Wilson said. "Chad's little mishap is not what we're here to talk about."

"It's not?" Andy asked. He sounded disappointed.

"It's not?" Chad repeated. He sounded hopeful.

"It's not," Dr. Wilson said. He sounded nervous.

The boys looked at their father, surprised. Had he ever been nervous before? He was usually very smooth and in control.

"What's up, Dad?" Andy asked.

"Well, did you boys pay attention to what Dr. Anderson shared tonight?" Dr. Wilson began. He saw Chad's head drop in shame and quickly went on. "I mean, did you catch what he was saying about Papua New Guinea? It's an island just north of Australia. Our church is growing like crazy there. The church runs a hospital and some health clinics in Papua New Guinea. Doctors also travel to villages and teach the people to take care of themselves. When the people learn some basic health care, they can prevent many diseases."

Andy jumped in with his usual goody-two-shoes comment. "Thanks for the recap, Dad. I didn't really catch all that at church."

Chad rolled his eyes at his brother. His dad went on. "There are lots of missionaries in Papua New Guinea trying to translate the Bible into the different languages of the country. But many of the people still have never heard God's Word."

"So what does that have to do with us, Dad?" Chad asked. "Are you wanting us to give some of our allowance to the cause or something?"

Dr. Wilson's eyes lit up, and Chad thought he had guessed correctly. No wonder his dad had been nervous. Chad immediately tried to figure out how small an offering he could get away with. After all, he had been saving to buy Land of the Locomquots II. There was no need to give up his computer game for people he didn't even know. Besides, these people lived halfway around the world.

Dr. Wilson seized on the word "give." "That's pretty close, Chad," Dr. Wilson said with a smile. "We've always made it a point to support missions with our money and our prayers." He looked at his wife and took a big breath before he continued, "I thought this time we could give of ourselves."

"Huh?" Chad and Andy asked at the same time.

Mrs. Wilson gave her husband a big smile. Dr. Wilson continued, "Your mother and I have talked this over. We'd like to move to Papua New Guinea for a year. We would go as temporary missionaries. I would travel and teach people how to prevent illnesses. We can help the translation teams distribute Bibles too. We would see for ourselves the missionaries and the church at work." He smiled at each of his sons. "It would be a great experience for all of us."

Chad sank back into the couch. The tornado in his head kept him from thinking clearly. Chuckles, his computer, his home—too many thoughts. "No, NO!" he yelled. "Anything else! I'll go in the smelly storage room for a month! Please!"

The rest of the family looked at each other in confusion. "What's this about the storage room?" Andy asked his parents.

"Beats me," Mrs. Wilson answered, looking at her husband with raised eyebrows.

"Don't look at me!" Dr. Wilson exclaimed. "I didn't mention the storage room!"

Chad buried his face in his hands and cried.

Chapter 4

"The spirits are fighting!" screamed one woman to another in her native language.

The women had been gathering vegetables from their gardens. Suddenly, screams and shouts erupted from the road leading into the village. The women dropped their tools and raced back toward their homes.

"Why would the spirits be angry?" cried one woman. "We give them sacrifices!"

When the women entered the village, they stopped dead in their tracks. Their eyes widened in disbelief. What they thought were the sounds of fighting were actually the sounds of celebrating. It took a minute to realize what they saw. Kosal was smiling and greeting his people. Cheers burst from the women's mouths as they ran to welcome their chief.

"You're alive!" the first woman shouted to Kosal. "You were healed by the spirits in Kudjip!"

"No," Kosal laughed, "by THE Spirit!"

The people were curious. Did he say there was only one spirit?

"Friends," said Kosal loudly in the language of his people, "I have much to tell you. But first, I must say 'thank you' for sending me to the hospital in Kudjip. It was a long journey. And it cost you the food of your gardens to send me on the airplane. But what I have learned is worth what you have paid."

Kosal began telling the story of his journey to Kudjip. When he got to the missionary hospital, the doctors prayed for him. In only a few hours, they knew why he was sick and gave him medicine for the illness. He was very sick for a week. But the doctors kept giving him medicine and praying for him. Soon he was feeling much better.

When Kosal told his people about how he got out of bed and was able to walk around, they cheered.

"Wait!" Kosal held up his hand. "I haven't told you the good news yet."

Confused looks covered their faces. There was even better news? Kosal kept talking. He told about the man from Dusin who had traveled to Kudjip with him. When Kosal began to get better, the man told him about a mighty Spirit.

When Kosal said this, the people flinched. Wasn't this what they had feared? What if the mighty Spirit had come back to destroy their village?

But Kosal kept talking. "In our village, we choose the most giving person as our leader. You have chosen me as your chief. But this Spirit loves you even more than I."

The people whispered to each other. They didn't understand what Kosal was saying.

Kosal held up a book. "This Book tells the story of the Spirit. The Spirit is God!"

The people gasped. They knew stories about God, but they also knew about Satan. Wasn't Satan more powerful than God? They had never heard about Jesus, so Kosal told them what he knew.

"In our village, we offer sacrifices to the spirits. We are afraid of them, so we try to make them happy. But God had a Son. His name was Jesus. And Jesus

loved us so much He gave himself as a sacrifice for us."

"A human sacrifice!" a man gasped.

"Yes," said Kosal. "But God is so powerful, Jesus didn't stay dead. And now we don't need to offer sacrifices anymore."

What the chief said was very hard for the people to understand. Kosal could tell by their faces that they wanted to hear more. He held up the Book again.

"This Book is not in our language. But I wanted it anyway. Though we cannot read it, we now have the story of God. Soon a man will come to our village. He will live with us and teach us what this Book says. We will no longer fear evil spirits. We will worship a loving Spirit!"

The people cheered when Kosal finished speaking. They had never dreamed of a good spirit. They knew only evil spirits. The people were always afraid. But a powerful Spirit who loved them? This was the best news they had ever heard!

Chapter 5

Chad stirred in his seat. The airplane was about to land in Papua New Guinea. Chad's stomach stirred. He could not settle his nerves. Papua New Guinea meant change. His dad had even started calling it PNG. Going to PNG meant saying good-bye to his home in the United States.

However, he did not leave his computer. Chad was happy his dad let him bring it. Dr. Anderson said the Wilsons would have a nice home in which to live. They would have electricity and running water. Using the computer wouldn't be a problem. And when his dad gave him Land of the Locomquots II for a going-away present, it made leaving a little easier.

Chad closed his eyes. He wished he was in his own chair in his own room back home. When he opened his eyes, he was still on the plane. Maybe this whole PNG trip was just one of his daydreams. A very bad daydream. He began to smile. Of course! It made much more sense. His father would never move the entire family across the world.

It was easy enough to dismiss the two days of plane rides as a dream. Chad had been pretty out of it after the first 10 hours or so. But this awful kink in his neck was not as easy to explain.

Chad felt someone tapping on his arm. "For goodness' sake, Chad!" his mom exclaimed. "Open your eyes! We're coming into Mount Hagen. We're HERE!"

Chad opened his eyes. He looked out the window next to his seat. Chad knew this was no daydream. Even his wild imagination could never have dreamed up anything so beautiful.

A rush of excitement went through his body. Yet he didn't want the others to see his excitement. He was determined to be unhappy in Papua New Guinea.

But the mountains were beautiful! They reached high into the sky, ending in jagged peaks. Their sides were lush and green. And the white clouds floated around them like beards on old men.

The plane dipped lower. Chad noticed that the green looked like patches on a quilt. He nudged his mom and pointed to them.

"Those must be gardens," she guessed.

The plane neared the runway and touched down. Chad's eyes grew wide with wonder. The plane coasted past grass huts. Surprised, Chad realized these were real. People actually lived in them!

The Wilsons walked down steps from the plane to the runway. They saw a fence lined with curious faces staring at them. Chad had never been the object of so much attention. He was afraid to stare back.

He already had many questions. What were those bags that so many women wore on their backs? Why was that old man almost naked? All he had were some leaves connected to a rope around his waist. Everyone else wore clothes, so why didn't he? Most of the women wore colorful tops that reached halfway to their knees. Under those they wrapped bright cloth around them to make a skirt. Chad got the impression that bright colors were more important here than clothes that matched.

Andy shifted his suitcase to his other hand and waved to the crowd. Chad was glad when the people smiled and waved back. He found himself smiling as well.

Chad's eyes were drawn to the one light face in the sea of dark faces. Soon that face started shouting, "Welcome, Wilsons!" The face was familiar. Anything familiar was welcome to Chad. When he heard the voice, it clicked. That was Wally the Wonder Walker!

Chapter 6

As the Wilsons rode away from their airport, there was another family standing on an airstrip deep in the rain forest. Levi and his wife, Ruth, stood quietly with their two young sons.

"Where is everybody, Papa?" asked Peta (PEET-uh).

"There should be someone from the village to meet us," said Levi to his oldest son.

This was not the welcome they had expected. Peta thought they would be welcomed with noises of celebration. All they heard was the buzz of their plane as it disappeared beyond a mountain.

"Hello?" called Levi into the jungle.

The only answer was the sound of the wind blowing across the runway.

They waited a while longer. Surely someone would show up. After a while, they decided to go on to the village. Peta and his family were from Papua New Guinea. But their new home was in an entirely different culture. The trees were different. The mountains were different. And he knew the customs and language of these people would be different. Peta was not too excited about coming. His father had explained to him the need to spread the Word of God. But Peta would still rather stay in his own village.

Eventually Peta and his family made it to the village. Where was everyone? Peta looked up at his dad.

The emptiness made his knees shake. His father looked around, concerned.

Just then a man came out of a hut and walked up to them.

"Levi?" asked the man.

Levi nodded.

"I am Kosal, the chief of this village."

It was hard to understand Kosal. He spoke a language that natives used to communicate between tribes. Peta knew the language, but Kosal had an accent.

"We tried to reach you before you came," Kosal said. "You can't stay here."

"What is wrong?" asked Levi. "We are here to help."

Kosal became angry. "I said you can't stay! Leave, now!"

Chapter 7

The Wilsons loaded into a van outside the airport. Dr. Anderson talked excitedly about how happy he was to have the Wilsons in PNG. He talked about the country as he shut the van doors, got in, and began to drive.

Chad stared out the window at the mountains, huts, and markets they drove past. Many of the native people used the road as a sidewalk. Then Dr. Anderson's voice got Chad's attention.

"In your last fax, you said you'd like your family to see life in the bush," he said. "Well, a good chance has come up. Just perfect for your family!"

"Great!" Dr. Wilson replied. "Tell us about it."

Dr. Anderson slowed the van to let a pig cross the road. "Well, we have a Papua New Guinea pastor named Levi. He is a missionary in a new area of this country. The village is way back in the bush. We'll have to take a plane part of the way. Then we'll walk for two days to get to where he is. This won't be a stroll in the park, either. It will be hard hiking. We have to cross two mountain ranges and about 30 streams and rivers."

Chad's smile disappeared. "On those rope bridges?" he asked.

Dr. Anderson was surprised Chad remembered his story. "Actually, Chad, most of these rivers are small enough to wade across," he answered. "And in this area, the bigger rivers have bridges made of logs."

Chad's smile returned. It would be cool to climb mountains and cross rivers in real life. He wouldn't have to just daydream about it.

"We will be walking through very isolated country. The people in Levi's village don't use cars or telephones. In some ways, it will be like traveling back in time. You will really get a feel of the way the whole country used to live." Dr. Anderson continued, "I will go with you as a guide. We will need some Papua New Guineans to help us too," he said. Dr. Anderson swerved the van around a pothole the size of a kitchen table. "We could spend a couple days with Levi and his family and then head back."

Dr. Wilson could hardly stay in his seat. He looked at his family. "What do you say, troops! Could we handle it?" he asked.

"Let's do it!" said Andy.

"Can we really, Dad?" asked Chad.

"If you think we're up to it, Darling, I'd love to try it!" said Mom.

"You need to know one more thing before you decide." Dr. Anderson became serious. "It's the reason we're going."

"What's that?" Dr. Wilson asked.

"Well, we received a radio message from a pastor a day's walk away from Levi's village. It was hard to figure out. All we could understand was that Levi and his family are having trouble. That could mean their children are sick. It could mean few people are listening to the gospel. Or it could mean . . . well, let's just say it could be serious. There probably won't be any danger, or I wouldn't suggest taking your family out there." Dr. Anderson slammed on his brakes to keep from hitting a child who darted across the street. "But in this type of setting, you have to realize there is always a chance of danger."

This time the Wilsons were not as quick to respond. Dr. Anderson grew quiet as well. For the rest of the drive, everyone quietly wondered what to do. They wondered whether or not they had the guts to make the trip.

Chapter 8

"Ouch!" Chad didn't even try to hide his pain or anger. This was the 50th time he had fallen. Andy turned around to look. Was that a grin on Andy's face? Chad reached for his glasses. They had fallen into the mud again.

The mud in Papua New Guinea was unlike any mud Chad had seen before. It was thick and sticky. Chad imagined it would be chewy if he tried to eat any. The mud sucked at his boots with each step. When it wasn't sucking at his feet, the mud was making him slip. Chad tried to explain to the others that the mud did not want him to go on. They could not understand.

Even his mother simply said, "Chad, you wanted to come on this hike. Keep moving." Thus, he kept plodding, slipping, and sliding his way along. Soon, he fell again. He took his time getting up.

He wiped his muddy glasses on his filthy T-shirt and put them on. No wonder he kept tripping. How was he supposed to see anything through these dirty glasses?

Chad ignored the hand that Andy offered to help him up. This hike was bad enough without having to get help from his brother. Just because Chad was 15 inches shorter than Andy, it did not mean that he was helpless. Still, what an awful hike!

Chad started up the mountain again. He brooded

every step of the way. He had always imagined mountain climbing to be fun. Boy, was he wrong! Why had he ever cast his vote for coming on this hike?

Chad wondered if it could really be true. Was he really hiking up a mountain in the middle of a rain forest? The closest he had been to nature was raking leaves. It was also hard to believe that he would be sleeping in some kind of grass hut. Everything about the rain forest amazed Chad. He saw trees so big around, the Wilson family car could drive through them. Splashes of red, purple, and orange blazed from the flowers of many plants. His mom's enthusiastic "Look at that flame of the forest!" drew his attention to a sweeping vine covered with red blossoms. Of course, Andy reacted with oohs and ahs.

The way Andy tried to be "mommy's pet" made Chad sick. Why was Andy always so perfect? Andy had never even had a pimple. Chad could not remember what life before acne had been like. Andy was strong and athletic. Chad was hopeless at sports.

"Weirdest of all," thought Chad, "Andy actually enjoys going to church." The services that Chad thought were boring and stale gave Andy energy and purpose. Chad knew his parents also enjoyed what they called their "relationship with God." He didn't feel like he really needed God. He was a good kid. And he had had a pretty decent life—until now.

Chad was happy to hear Dr. Anderson say, "Let's take a break." It was Dr. Anderson's job to make sure the Wilsons didn't get lost in the middle of the jungle. He also reminded them to drink lots of water. Most of all, he was encouraging. He kept assuring the group that they could make it, even when Chad felt too tired to go on.

The Wilsons, Dr. Anderson, and the three Papua New Guineans sat down. They removed snacks from their waist packs. Chewing on beef jerky and trail mix, they talked about the beauty around them. After a while, their talk came to World War II planes scattered throughout the mountains. "You mean there are actual planes?" Chad asked excitedly. The thought of seeing a piece of history in real life thrilled him.

"Yes, Chad, there are a few planes. My son found a bullet at a plane we went to see last year," Dr. Anderson answered.

Jerry, one of the guides, said something in Pidgin (PI-jin). Dr. Anderson translated for the Wilsons. Jerry told about the remains of a plane near his village. It went down before he was born. His parents had told him about it. They had never seen an airplane before. The villagers had thought it was from the spirit world. No one would get close to it.

"Hey, I remember reading about a battle on the coast of Papua New Guinea!" Andy said. "The Papua New Guineans were very helpful to the Allies. The Australians called them angels. They helped carry the wounded to safety."

Dr. Anderson stood and stretched. "Well, it's been good to rest. But we better get going. I want us to reach the halfway point before dark."

As they started walking again, Chad began daydreaming. He dreamed he was Lieutenant Wilson, a World War II military pilot. He had been flying a mission over Papua New Guinea when he hit a heavy rainstorm. Without enough fuel to turn back, he tried an emergency landing. Miraculously, he survived.

Chad had crawled from the pile of metal that had once been a P-39 plane. He found himself surrounded

by dark, sinister faces. These people weren't like the "angels" his soldier friends had met. They bound his hands behind his back and led him on a death march. They pushed and shoved him up and down more mountains than he could count. The muscles in his legs burned and cramped. Despite his cries for mercy, his enemies kept pushing him onward. Only once had they stopped for a break.

Lieutenant Wilson knew he would soon meet his death. He must escape. But how? There were seven of them. They would easily overpower him if he tried anything foolish. As they hiked on, he kept his mind alert. He looked for any chance to make a run for it.

When the group at last stopped to make camp, Chad saw his chance. They unbound his hands and showed that they wanted him to help gather wood for a fire. Chad wandered slowly into a nearby clearing. He picked up some wood as he went. He did not want to draw attention to himself. To his surprise and relief, his captors began to talk among themselves. Then the relief gave way to fear. Were they planning something? Would they sacrifice him to an evil spirit? Was he gathering wood for a fire that he was meant to die in?!

There might not be another chance. He had to try to make it on his own in the jungle. It would be better than certain death at the hands of his captors. He turned and picked his way through the thick jungle. He was careful not to leave any signs. He didn't want his captors to find him.

Chapter 9

Chad was caught up in his daydream. He had no idea of the danger he was getting himself into. The light in the forest was fading.

The other members of the camp did not realize Chad was gone. Chad's father and the other men in the group were building a shelter. They were busy chopping down the trees and palm leaves they would use to build it. His mother was busy making a meal for eight. She thought Chad was gathering firewood. She had asked him to do it.

Meanwhile, Chad crept through the thick grass. His legs moved as fast as possible. Putting distance between himself and his captors was of most importance. There was no trail for them to follow. He would be hard to find. Still, he continued to push himself. He wasn't afraid of the jungle. He was Lieutenant Wilson, a military officer trained to survive.

Chad did not notice the creeping darkness. He thought about his plan. "OK, I've got a canteen with water. If I find a river, I can fill it up. I've got a belt pack with some beef jerky and peanuts. I better try to make that last."

Thinking about his supplies made his stomach rumble. "When did my captors last let me stop and eat? It must have been HOURS ago." He was glad he was his own boss. He could eat and rest whenever he wanted. "I'll just walk a little more. When I'm sure they can't find me, I'll stop for some dinner," he thought.

As Chad climbed over a large rock, he decided he would allow himself three peanuts. He also ate part of a piece of beef jerky. Two sips from the canteen washed it all down. He planned for his supplies to last him six or seven meals. Surely the Allies would find him by then.

He came to a tree that had fallen over. The stump was still in the ground. It looked like a good place to rest. His weary legs and growling stomach persuaded him to do so. The seat felt rough and uneven. It was not as comfortable as it looked. But it was better than sitting on the ground.

In no time, he dug into his pack. His stomach growled as he ripped off a piece of the beef jerky. He smacked it with delight. Then he popped the three peanuts into his mouth. The salty taste of both made him thirsty. He took more than just two sips. Mealtime did not last long enough. Chad's stomach rumbled angrily.

His big plans to stretch out his supplies lost their importance. It would probably be OK if he had a little extra just this once. "After all," he thought, "I worked harder today than I ever have before."

He decided to eat and hike at the same time. His captors still might be too close. He stood and stretched his tired legs. Sharp pains ran up and down his calves. His steps were not as fast as before. He did not want to slip. Getting mud on his jerky would not be fun. However, eventually he did fall and land in the awful mud. Thankfully, his snack was clenched between his teeth. Not a speck of mud landed on it.

Chad climbed to his feet and kept walking. He

didn't notice how quickly his beef jerky was disappearing. He was too busy thinking about his escape. Before long, he finished the first piece and chewed on the second. His water supply worried him the most. What if he didn't find a river? In survival stories, he had always heard that water was important.

Chad felt a drop of rain land on the middle of his forehead. Then there were a few drops. Soon water poured down in a deafening roar.

It was probably good that Chad still thought he was Lieutenant Wilson. As an air force pilot, he had more guts than he did as a little boy. He began to plan.

"I'd better stop and find shelter. Maybe I can do something with some vines or some of the big palm leaves," he said aloud, trying to build his confidence. It was hard to move in his wet, heavy jeans. The fog on his glasses made it hard to see.

The palm leaves came loose with ease. He planned to use them for a roof. Next, he needed branches for support. There were none strong enough within his reach. He looked around for more. He made out the shapes of a cluster of trees in the darkness. His boots slid and sloshed in the mud. He found a low branch and pulled on it. But it did not want to come off. He tightened his grip and jerked backward. His feet shot out from under him. He burst through the trees and felt the ground disappear under his feet.

Chapter 10

Peta screamed and fell on the ground in pain.

Levi ran to his son. Peta held his foot and rolled back and forth on the jungle floor. Tears streamed down his face as his father tried to comfort him.

Peta and his father had been collecting scraps of sugarcane to boil for dinner. Peta had seen a large piece on the ground. But when he ran for it, a four-inch sliver of bamboo sliced into his bare heel.

"Aaaaahhh!" screamed Peta as his father removed the splinter.

Levi wiped the blood from Peta's heel and held his shirt over the wound. "Are you OK, Son?"

"It's better since you took it out," Peta sniffed. Then in frustration he snapped, "It's not fair!"

"What's not fair?" Levi asked.

"How come all we ever eat is sugarcane and left-over vegetables?"

"Peta, we can't take food from these people's gardens. That would be stealing. The vegetables and sugarcane they discard are the only ones we can take," said Levi.

"Well, how come we stay here? These people don't want us. Kosal told us to leave. I want to go home."

"I believe these people want us here, but they are afraid of the witch doctors," said Levi.

"But Kosal was the one who asked us to come. Why won't he welcome us?"

"Kosal doesn't know much about Christ. The doctors at the hospital helped him come to know Jesus, but Kosal's faith is weak. The witch doctors have told these people Satan will kill them if they listen to our words about God. It's hard for these people to believe that God is more powerful than Satan."

"But why do we stay?" asked Peta.

"I believe God wants us to stay," said Levi. "These people need to hear about Him. I have told Kosal we will stay until God tells us to leave."

"What did Kosal say about that?"

"He said we can do what we want. But we can't have any food from the village. So we have to look out here in the jungle for things the villagers don't want," explained Levi.

"That's why we always boil sugarcane for dinner, huh?" said Peta.

"Yes, Son. And I know you are always hungry. But you are healthy. The Lord is taking care of us."

Chapter 11

Chad covered his face as he flew down the mountain. Wet branches slapped his bare skin. He slid over roots and rocks. "Oh, God!" he cried. "Please HELP! I don't want to DIE!" The words poured from Chad's mouth. He didn't even realize he was praying.

As soon as the words were out, the falling sensation stopped. Chad's body felt like a stretched rubber band snapping back into place. He wasn't falling anymore—but wait. He hadn't hit the ground either.

He was hanging—his body folded almost in half, with his nose close to his knees. His hands and feet dangled weakly. Something, or Someone, had caught him. Was that God holding him by his belt loop? It sure felt like it!

"Oh, WOW! Thanks, God!" Chad exclaimed. "Oh, man. OK, You really convinced me. I know I haven't paid much attention to You before now. But I'm listening. Don't let go, OK? Please, God, just DON'T LET GO!"

Chad slowly let out a big breath. OK. God wasn't letting go. Now what? He slowly opened his eyes. It was pitch black! He had been so busy he hadn't even noticed nighttime coming. Chad's heart began to beat even faster.

"OK, God, thanks for hanging on. Now, if You don't mind, maybe You could put me down—nice and easy. Not that I'm complaining, but this isn't the most comfortable position. It's getting pretty cold too. Yep, just put me down on the ground, OK? God?"

Chad's newfound faith started to get shaky. Why wasn't he moving? He was still hanging up here in space. He began to slowly move one hand toward his belt loop. After all, it was dark. Maybe God had fallen asleep. If he could just reach back there and tap God's hand, maybe he could wake Him up. What a thought!

What would God's hand feel like? Chad found his belt loop. Sure enough, there was something round poking through it. Was that God's finger? It was hard and rough! It felt like—a tree branch.

Chad let out the breath he had been holding. What a disappointment! God hadn't caught him after all. It was just a silly old tree branch.

Of course, he was glad the branch had caught him, but it just wasn't the same. It meant he was alone out here, hanging in space. He was soaked and felt lonely, not to mention that he might be hundreds of feet from the ground!

Hundreds of feet? Oh, no. Chad began to sweat. The thought fueled his active imagination. What if he was dangling over the edge of a cliff? It could be as large as the ones he had seen on his hike. Some looked to be a mile high. At the bottom, there was probably a rocky river. He thought he could hear the roar of the rapids even from this distance.

Chad pictured the limb snapping. He could see himself falling down the steep cliff and splattering on a jagged rock. It was not a pretty picture. At best, every bone in his body would be broken! If there were a river, how could he swim to safety with crushed arms and legs?

For once, Chad made an effort to control his daydreaming. He made himself stop thinking about the fall. He realized he would just have to wait until the sun came up to see where he was. Then he could make a plan.

Chad concentrated. He tried to think of something good. "At least the rain has stopped," he realized. "I wonder when that happened. Plus there's not much wind. That's good! If a good wind came along, it could knock me right off this branch!"

Chad's mind pictured the wind blowing him from his fragile position, like a leaf blowing from a tree branch. His heart beat faster at the thought when a breeze lifted the front of his hair. He tensed every muscle as the breeze grew stronger. It became a powerful gust. Chad heard a sickening "creeeeaaak" as the limb that supported him began to crack.

"No!" was all he had time to yell.

Chapter 12

Chad felt a fog lift from his brain. He became aware of serious pain. He tried to figure out from where the pain was coming. It was hard to pinpoint. Every part of his body ached.

He tried to remember what had happened. He had fallen over a cliff, and a tree branch saved him. Oh, yes, then the wind had started to blow. The branch had made a sickening sound.

Eyes still closed, Chad searched his memory. Of course, he had fallen when the branch broke. However, he couldn't remember anything after the wind blew. Had he passed out when the tree branch started to break? Well, that was probably for the best. Who wants to remember what it's like to fall thousands of feet?

Enough of the past; what should he do now? Was he splattered on that jagged rock he had imagined? Was every bone broken? How would he ever get help out here in the middle of nowhere?

He didn't hear the roaring water that had been part of his daydream. He didn't feel splattered. He wasn't all spread out. In fact, he felt like . . . like he was hanging by his belt loop!

With a shock, Chad realized he hadn't fallen. He still hung in space. The sound of the branch creaking must have caused him to pass out. It must not have broken after all. All this pain must be from spending the night in this horrible position.

That meant the fall was still to come! How else could he ever get down from here? His body shivered at the thought. His eyes shut tighter. The red glow of sunlight filtered through his eyelids. He did not want to see the drop below him.

Chad talked to himself. "OK, Chad, you've gotta open your eyes. I know it's tough. You're gonna freak out, OK? It's gonna be a long way down. But if you don't look, you'll never find a way out of this." Chad stopped and thought. Then he added, "Hey, God, if You're out there somewhere, can You give me a hand with this?"

He began to count aloud to give himself courage. "One . . . two . . . three!" He opened his eyes. A yell burst from his mouth.

Chapter 13

"PRAISE THE LORD!!!"

Chad didn't know if he should laugh or cry. The ground was just three feet below him! It wasn't a mile-long drop. It wasn't the jagged rock. It wasn't a rushing river. It was just green grass. It even looked soft!

Chad slowly breathed a sigh of relief. Wow.

He reached back and found his belt loop. Carefully, he unhooked himself and dropped to the ground. Before he straightened up, he patted the earth. It was good to be standing on solid ground. He plucked a piece of the tall grass and ran it through his fingers. He had survived the worst ordeal of his life.

Chad began to look around. He looked behind him and saw where he had fallen. It wasn't a cliff at all, but a steep hill. It was about 30 feet high. It wasn't the mile-high cliff he had imagined. Still, Chad thought it was pretty impressive. It was slick and muddy. He could see the trail of branches and weeds he had crushed in his fall. "Wow, no wonder I'm so scratched up!" he exclaimed, looking from the cliff to his battered arms. He took time to admire his impressive wounds. "After all," he thought, "it's not every day that you fall over a cliff!"

When he finished admiring his injuries, Chad felt tough enough to attack the cliff. "You're not getting the best of me, you big pile of dirt!" he boasted. He stretched his scratched, bruised arms toward a branch

and grabbed on. His muscles ached with the effort. Half pulling himself and half walking, he tried to move up the side of the cliff. But every time he did, his hiking boots slid back down. Finally, he found a foothold. He let go of the branch with one hand and reached for another a few feet up. But the first branch snapped, and he found himself on his back on the ground. The broken limb was still in his hand. "Boy," he said to the limb, "I'm glad you're not the branch that caught me last night!"

Chad got up and decided to try again. But the mud was simply too slick, and the branches weren't strong enough. He couldn't make any progress. So he sat where he had fallen again and looked up at the cliff. He sadly admitted that he could not climb back up.

He began to work through his problems aloud. "If I can't climb this cliff, how will I get back to the camp? How will I find Mom and Dad?" At once, he remembered what he had done. "Oh, Dad! Mom! Andy! I LEFT THEM! I was daydreaming, and I wandered off! Oh no!" He felt that familiar feeling of failure he always felt after another daydream-turned-disaster. His stomach churned. His insides felt twisted. The feeling spread from inside outward, until his fingers and toes tingled.

"I'm by myself out here in the middle of the jungle in Papua New Guinea! How will I ever get back? Even if I could get up this cliff, then what? I wouldn't have a clue where to go!"

Chad's eyes filled with tears. He cried harder than he had when Andy erased Land of the Locomquots from the computer. It wiped out the record that said Chad had beaten Andy's score.

Chad cried until he used up all his tears. It made him feel a little better. Then the sensation in his stomach began to change. He heard it rumble and realized he was terribly hungry. He reached for his bag. At least he could comfort himself with some of his rations.

He unzipped the pack and looked inside. His eyebrows came together. His forehead wrinkled. He knew he had made rules for himself about how much he could eat. He also knew he had cheated some yesterday. But had he gotten this carried away? Could what he was seeing really be true?

Not only was Chad alone in the jungle of Papua New Guinea, but also his pack was empty! He had no food!

Chapter 14

Chad licked his lips. His mouth was very dry. He felt as if he had been eating sandpaper. Landing in that rushing river would not have been so bad after all. So what if he had broken a few bones? There would have been plenty to drink.

Chad searched for any sign of water. He needed it to survive. But where? Where should he even begin his search? He thought of the rain the night before. It seemed like a cruel joke that he was so thirsty now. Where had all that water gone?

That question gave Chad an idea. He looked back up at the trail his body had carved into the mountainside. A trickle of water ran down through the mud. He followed the glistening water all the way down to the bottom of the cliff. "Aha!" he exclaimed. The trickle didn't fall into a muddy puddle. Instead, it joined another barely noticeable ribbon of water. It moved slowly from left to right along the wall of the cliff. At last he knew which way he must go.

Chad followed his sparkling trail. He decided to see how many interesting objects he could see as he walked along.

It was good that he was paying attention to his surroundings. About 10 feet ahead and to the right of his path, something looked at him. It was at least 5 feet tall because it was taller than Chad. Its head was bright blue and purple. Black hair covered its body.

Chad caught his breath and froze. He realized he was looking at a cassowary (KAS-uh-wer-ee)—the world's most dangerous bird.

He remembered what his dad had said about them. A cassowary can kill a person with a swift kick of its claws.

Chad remained frozen. He was afraid to even breathe. He did not know what else to do. The bird looked at him for a few moments. Then it turned and ran into the bushes. To Chad's amazement, the bird easily jumped over a four-foot palm tree that was in its path. It was as frightened as Chad was.

"Wow!" Chad exclaimed, letting out the breath he had been holding. "Oh, wow." He wiped the sweat off his forehead. His hands were shaking. He rested for a moment, then moved on.

Chad's exhaustion and fear added to his clumsiness. He tried to keep his eyes wide open. While he scanned ahead for danger, he did not see a low-hanging branch right in front of him. The collision against his forehead brought him to his knees.

"Ow!" he cried, reaching up to check the damage. His dirty fingers felt something wet and sticky. He lowered his hand and looked at the blood. It wasn't much, really—probably just a scratch. At this point, though, it was more than he could take. Now his head throbbed with the rest of his body.

"So, is it a contest now, God?" he yelled to the sky above him. "Behind door A: Chad gets to BLEED TO DEATH! Behind door B: STARVE TO DEATH! Or door C: DIE OF THIRST!" Chad was sobbing, barely able to get the words out.

Something strange began to happen as Chad finished his outburst. He realized he was no longer sob-

bing. He was laughing hysterically. He knew he didn't have much to laugh about, but he couldn't stop. His shoulders shook, and tears streamed down his face. It felt so good to laugh! How long had it been since he had thought anything was funny? He laughed so hard his stomach began to cramp. Then he laughed even harder.

As Chad laughed, his attitude improved. He thought, "If I can laugh NOW, I can get through anything." His fear began to disappear. A sense of peace filled him. He realized that the peace was from God. Again, Chad felt as if he wasn't alone.

"So You listen to me, even when I'm being a brat?" he prayed. He felt ashamed that he had been so cheeky. "I'm glad You are with me. I really need You now."

Chad got back on his feet. His journey went smoothly for a little over an hour. But while he day-dreamed about fighting off the cassowary, he stumbled over a root. His hands scrambled to keep from falling. His glasses flew off his face.

He felt through the tall grass for his glasses. Without them he was practically blind. Broken tree limbs lay scattered around. He carefully moved them aside. A huge one sat in his path. When he grabbed the limb, it slithered through his hands. Chad jumped back and watched the limb slide into a thicket. It must have been 6 feet long.

Chad reviewed all he knew about the snakes of the rain forest. He remembered that pythons live there. And they can grow up to 20 feet long. Thankfully the snake he saw wasn't that big.

With a shiver, Chad imagined the snake striking at him. Then he remembered that pythons don't bite.

Chad put his hand to his throat and imagined the snake squeezing him.

"As much as I'd like a hug right now, I think I'll pass on one from a python!" he exclaimed. "Surely, I did not just try to pick one up. I make dumb mistakes, but even I'm not THAT clumsy."

Chad squinted and stared into the grass where the snake had disappeared. What if it came back? He wished he had his glasses so he could see better. But he did not feel like poking around in the grass anymore.

He bowed his head to pray, and a glare flashed in his eye. His glasses! He picked them up and put them on. Then he prayed a prayer of thankfulness.

Chad stood and walked back to the side of the mountain. He was surprised at how much water was flowing along the path. It had increased gradually as he had hiked along. Chad's spirit lifted. He kept walking.

At last the brook did what Chad had hoped it would do. It led him to a real, refreshing, sparkling river! Chad gave a whoop of delight. He ran to it, licking his parched lips.

He didn't stop when he reached the river. The cool water swirled around his knees. It almost knocked him over. His feet dug into the sand to keep his balance. Splashes of joy wrinkled the smooth surface of the water. He acted like a three-year-old in a backyard wading pool. Finally he pushed his mouth into the cool water. It was fantastic!

He drank until he couldn't drink any more. Then he filled his canteen. After it was full, he went back to the bank of the river. A big, flat rock stuck out of the water. Its warmth soothed his muscles as he rested on it.

He sunned himself like a kitten. A peace fell over him for the moment. But after a while, an uncomfortable feeling grew around his ankles. Was it an itch or a sting? He reached down to scratch. But it didn't help. He pulled the leg of his jeans up and bent over to look—"AAAACH!!!"

It was a little thing. Only about half an inch long. It was shaped like the paisleys that decorated his dad's favorite tie. But Chad realized that the tiny thing was a leech, and it was sucking his blood! He gathered his courage, yanked it off, and flung it into the river. Shivers of disgust ran up and down Chad's body. He wanted to get away from the water. He walked back into the jungle and found a tree stump to sit on.

At last Chad gave up. How could he get anywhere? He didn't even know which direction to walk. He was lost.

Chapter 15

Chad put his face in his hands. But he didn't cry. He didn't have any tears left. He needed to make a plan. He tried to concentrate.

After a few minutes, a noise startled him. It sounded as if something was moving through the bushes.

For a moment, he thought he had been found. His face lit up with hope. But the hope drained away. If it was his dad or Dr. Anderson, wouldn't someone be calling his name?

Chad froze. What kind of wild animal could it be? Had he survived this long, only to be eaten by a wild pig? Or had the cassowary returned to finish him off? Whatever it was, it sounded as if it was headed directly toward Chad.

He looked around and found a tree with low branches. It was slippery from the rain. Chad tried to climb it. But he wasn't getting very far. The noise came closer and closer. He gave up on climbing any higher and snuggled up to the trunk of the tree. His feet balanced on the lowest branch. With eyes closed, he waited for the attack.

The suspense was terrible. It sounded as if the thing whacked down grass and bushes as it cleared its path to Chad. The creature must be huge and strong! Frantically, Chad tried to remember if Papua New Guinea had bears. It sure sounded like a bear.

When the noise stopped just below Chad's branch, he held his breath. The sound of heavy breathing reached Chad's ears. Maybe it wouldn't see him. Chad hoped it would start walking again. Then it grabbed his ankle. "Aaaagh!" Chad screamed. "Aaaagh! Aaaaagh! God, PLEASE HELP ME!" He hugged the tree so tightly that the bark scratched his face.

He finally stopped screaming to get a breath. But the screaming continued. Chad was confused. If he wasn't screaming, who was? And why wasn't he being torn to shreds by huge, hairy claws?

At last he opened his eyes and looked down. He saw a set of big black eyes in a face that looked a lot like his. The boy's face was full of fear. He had stopped screaming too. This was no wild animal. It was only a Papua New Guinean boy. He looked the same age as Chad.

When Chad realized his screams had scared the boy, he felt bad. "Hey, I'm sorry. It's OK, really. I won't hurt you." The boy tilted his head and stared. He hadn't seen very many boys who looked like Chad.

Chad realized the boy might be able to help him. He didn't want to let him get away. He smiled at him as he slowly climbed down from his branch. "Can I go to your house?" he asked.

The little boy just stared at him. "Oh! You probably can't speak English!" Chad guessed. "Let's see if I can remember Pidgin. I had a few lessons. Um. Me like go long house belong you." Chad knew it wasn't perfect. He was relieved when the little boy's face lit up. Apparently Chad had gotten his point across. The boy motioned for Chad to follow.

They set out in a new direction. With each step, the boy whacked the tall grass and bushes with the bush knife he carried. Chad smiled. He could never have imagined anything like this. He also thought about what an unusual place Papua New Guinea was. Chad would have never been allowed to carry a huge knife like that at home. His mother still reminded him not to run while holding scissors!

The boy talked excitedly in Pidgin. He talked so fast that Chad couldn't understand him. Still, Chad felt as if he had found a friend. It was the best feeling he had had in two days!

Not far down the path, Chad tripped over a tree root and fell. The boy laughed hysterically. Chad's face turned red with embarrassment and anger. He thought the boy was proud of how easily he could move through the rough terrain. The second time Chad fell, he surprised himself by laughing too. He decided the boy wasn't making fun of him. Chad's clumsiness just amused him.

Before long, they reached a path. The path was rough, though. Chad had to keep his eyes on the ground so he would not fall.

Chad didn't look up until he heard the boy say, "House belong me." Then Chad caught his breath at the beauty before him.

He saw a house made out of bamboo. The bamboo was cut and woven together in a pretty pattern that made strong walls. Grass lay on top to make a roof. Smoke drifted up through the grass of the roof. The tiny, white clouds rode the breeze. It was a house like most in Papua New Guinea.

What made Chad gasp was the beauty of the setting. The house was on the edge of a tall hill. There was a jagged mountain to the right. Flowers in vivid reds and yellows sat around the house. Many different types of trees provided shade for the area. Their leaves were a vibrant green. It was a beautiful place for a house. Especially one made of bamboo.

Chad's eyes soaked in the beautiful sight. He wished he had a camera with him. He thought of amusement parks he had seen decorated like a jungle. He had always thought they looked pretty real. Now he realized how fake they were.

Chad smiled at his new friend. The boy ran ahead and yelled to everyone in the house to come see what he had found. A man, a lady, and a younger boy came out. They looked even more surprised to see Chad than the boy had! Chad was surprised when the man said, "Well, hello!" in English.

"Hello!" Chad answered. He was glad to be able to speak his own language.

"I see you have met my son Peta. I am Levi," said the man. "Peta said he found you in a tree. Are you lost?" the man asked. He was concerned that Chad was alone in this remote area.

"Yes," Chad said. He cleared his throat to get the words out. "I was with my family, but I got lost. Can you help me?" Tears began rolling down his face.

The lady came forward and wiped Chad's tears with her dress. She held him close to her side and stroked his face. Her hand was hard and rough like sandpaper. Still, Chad found it soothing. Then she led him inside the house.

She bent low to get through the door and didn't straighten up when she got inside. Chad wondered why until he felt the stinging in his eyes. The upper half of the room was full of smoke. It came from a fire in the middle of the floor. He looked up. The grass roof was blackened. He didn't see a hole or a chimney. No wonder it was so smoky! The smell reminded Chad of summer camp.

A big pot hung over the fire. Chad's stomach let out a roar of hunger. He realized that the pot must hold supper. He'd heard missionaries talk about cau cau (KOW KOW), a type of sweet potato, and taro (TAR-oh), a root Papua New Guineans liked to eat. Chad hadn't been excited about trying them at the time. Now he found himself hoping the pot was full of either!

Once Chad sat down inside, he told the family his story. He finished with, "I may never see my family again!"

Chapter 16

"Oh, yes, you will!" said a deep voice from the doorway.

"DAD!" Chad yelled. His father's head peeped through the door. Chad burst out of the hut and into Dr. Wilson's arms. The rest of the Wilsons crowded around him. Chad was even glad to see Andy.

Tears flowed down Dr. Wilson's face. "Chad, Chad, what happened?"

"It was my fault!" Mrs. Wilson said. "I shouldn't have sent you out for wood."

"No, it was my fault, really," Chad insisted. "I was—"

"Wait, wait," said Dr. Anderson. "I don't want to ruin this beautiful reunion. But why don't we all get some food and rest? Then we will share our stories."

"Good idea!" Chad agreed. "Oh yeah, everybody, you've got to meet my new friends." Chad introduced everyone as they greeted each other.

When the introductions were over, Levi's wife, Ruth, stepped forward. "Won't all of you please join our family for supper. Dr. Anderson, you know I enjoy having guests."

"Oh, yes, Ruth! I've been telling the Wilsons what a fine hostess you are. You're known for having plenty of tasty food ready for unexpected guests. I see tonight is no different." Dr. Anderson said. He saw the big pot heating over the fire and licked his lips.

Chad's eyes followed the missionary's gaze. His stomach roared happily at the thought of all that food. He did not know that Dr. Anderson already knew these people. "Of course," he thought, "Dr. Anderson does lots of wandering around out here. Maybe he knows just about everyone."

"There's something I must tell you," Ruth said, interrupting Chad's thoughts. "We don't have much food tonight. Sugarcane was all we could get. The boys found it in the rain forest. I'm boiling it now. We'll be happy to share what we have. I'm just sorry there isn't more."

"What? There's no food?" Dr. Anderson asked. "Ruth, Levi, how can this be? Has someone destroyed your garden?"

Levi answered, "No, no one has destroyed it. The village hasn't let us plant a garden. But I guess our story can wait too. Come and sit by the fire. Ruth," Levi chuckled, "will you get each of our guests a bowl of our specialty, sugar soup?"

Despite Levi's laughing, Dr. Wilson remained serious. "Goodness," he said, "there's no need for us to eat up all your food. We don't have much left after two days on the trail. But we can share what we do have."

So the group began to file into the hut. They all found places to sit around the fire. The little hut was almost bursting. Still, everyone was happy to be together. It felt like a party.

The doctors passed around bits of beef jerky and trail mix. They made sure they saved enough for the trip home. Dr. Anderson produced several packages of noodles. Ruth added them to the soup. They all talked at top speed while they waited. Finally, it was time to eat. Chad's stomach gurgled as he took a drink. The soup tasted funny. But Chad did not care. He drank more, then asked for seconds.

Soon the pot was empty. Maybe story time would take their minds off food. The group agreed that Levi should share his story first. "After all," Dr. Anderson said, "you're the reason we're all here."

"What?" Chad asked. He wasn't being proud. But he thought he was the reason they were all together.

Mrs. Wilson explained, "He means that Levi's problems are the reason we are here. We would not have come if everything were OK."

"How did you know he was having problems?" asked Chad. "Wait a minute. You mean Levi is the pastor we're worried about? This was where we were headed?"

Andy rolled his eyes. "Chad, do you ever hear anything? Didn't you pay attention during our orientation for this trip?"

Dr. Wilson jumped into the conversation quickly. "Andy, that will be enough. Now please, Levi, do share with us. What has been happening in your village?"

Chad felt the heat of the hut fade. Levi's low voice captured his attention, as he told what had happened in Kosal's village.

When Levi finished talking, Dr. Anderson spoke. "Let's stop and pray right now for this village," he said, "and for Levi. Prayer is the best weapon in spiritual warfare."

They bowed their heads and began to pray. Every once in a while Chad opened his eyes and looked around. He wasn't sure what to think. These people

didn't sound as if they were reciting something they had memorized. They weren't just listing all the sick people they knew. They weren't asking God to give them things. They were praying with power, asking God to work in hearts in this village. They were talking to God as if they knew Him personally.

Chad began to feel an ache inside. It was a longing to know God personally, as these people did. "Maybe in a way, I'm still lost," he thought to himself.

The group finished their prayer meeting. Chad was embarrassed to find many eyes focusing on him. "Chad," his dad said, "we're so thrilled to have you back! You've survived a night and a day on your own in the rain forest. Why don't you tell us what it was like?"

Chapter 17

Chad did not want to admit the reason he had gotten lost. But he did anyway. "I wandered off while collecting wood. I daydreamed that I was a downed fighter pilot. Eventually, I realized I was alone. I couldn't believe it!"

Chad told about the rainstorm. Dr. Anderson said the storm kept them from finding him. When Chad told about falling over the cliff, his mother began to cry. Chad shared how he had cried out to God. His cheeks turned red as he admitted, "For a minute I actually thought God did catch me. Then I realized it was just a silly tree branch."

"What?" Dr. Anderson interrupted. "You don't think God was there when that happened to you? I believe you were right the first time."

"I guess that does make sense," Chad said, smiling. "Maybe I wasn't alone out there after all."

Chad revealed how terrified he had been, hanging there in the dark. He did not know how far from the ground he might be. When he told them how far he really was, they all had a good laugh.

"Don't you see, Chad? You prayed and asked for God's help," said Chad's father. "All you had to do was open your eyes. Again, God helped you."

Chad thought about what his dad and Dr. Anderson said. Then he continued his story. Here in the cozy hut, his experiences did not sound as terrifying. He enjoyed being the star of the group.

Chad told about the "wild animal" he heard coming through the brush. Everyone in the room, especially Peta, was rigid with fright. Chad revealed that Peta had been the "animal." Peta shrieked with laughter.

Chad didn't wait for anyone to comment this time. He shared, "That's another time I prayed, and God heard me. He must have sent Peta to find me. Peta, you saved my life!"

Peta beamed with pride.

"What a beautiful missionary story!" Levi exclaimed. "Peta, you'll make a great missionary someday!"

"What do you mean?" Chad asked.

"I believe I see what Levi means," Chad's mom said. "Do you really understand why we came to Papua New Guinea, Chad?"

"So Dad could help the doctors at the hospital and village clinics," Chad answered.

"That's part of it," Dr. Wilson admitted, "but the bigger picture is to do what Peta did for you."

Chad didn't get it. "Find kids lost out in the rain forest? How many are out there?"

"Thousands, Chad," Dr. Anderson said. "Not just kids, either—mothers and fathers too. They all need someone to unite them with their HEAVENLY Father."

At last Chad understood. "When you decided to come here, Dad, and help these people find God, well . . ." Chad paused. He looked down at the dirt floor he was sitting on.

"Yes, Chad?" said his father.

"Did you ever think your own son would be one of them?" Chad gained courage. "Dad, I think I'd like to pray."

Shouts of "Hallelujah!" and "Praise the Lord!" erupted. They filled the hut and went into the night air. The group prayed together for the second time that night. For the second time that day, Chad was found.

Chapter 18

The excitement of the evening made it hard to settle down. Chad felt as if a burden had lifted off his shoulders. For the first time in his life he felt peace.

The small hut and large group made it impossible for everyone to sleep inside. Some of the men went outside with Dr. Anderson. They built lean-tos from palm leaves. Chad teasingly reminded them not to fall off the mountain while selecting their branches.

Levi and his wife insisted that the Wilsons sleep on their bed for the night. Dr. Wilson didn't want the couple to have to sleep on the ground. But he couldn't convince them otherwise.

The bed wasn't like Chad's at home. Instead, it was like a queen-sized bench built into the wall. It was made from woven grass. Wood gave it support. The Wilsons spread their sleeping bags over it. Then they snuggled into the small space. Andy slept next to the wall. In the middle lay Chad and Dr. Wilson. Mrs. Wilson balanced on the edge. "I think the tree branch was roomier," Chad joked.

"Yeah, we're glad to have you back, Chad. But I didn't think we'd have to be *this* close," Andy responded.

"Chad," Dr. Wilson said in a serious voice, "we are glad to have you back. I want you to know I'm proud of you. I'm proud of the decision you made.

And I'm proud of how you handled yourself in the rain forest."

"Seriously!" Andy agreed. "I don't know if I would have made it out there, little brother. You did really well."

Chad smiled. He would rather be smashed between family members than hanging from a tree branch any day. Then he drifted off to sleep.

* * *

Shouts pierced the early morning air. Chad jolted upright into a sitting position. He sat still, trying to hear what was going on. The shouts turned to chanting. He did not understand a single word. His parents and brother were sitting up as well.

"What's going on?" Andy asked, his voice a little shaky.

The chanting sounded excited. It was hard to tell if the voices were angry or happy.

Chad was afraid. He imagined the villagers dancing around a pot. Inside the pot sat Levi and his family. Was Chad's family going to be next?! Chad's stomach rumbled. He clutched it. This was no time to think about food. Chad jumped when he heard Levi shout.

"Dr. Wilson! Boys! Come quickly!"

"You might want to stay here, Darling. Let us find out what's going on," Dr. Wilson said to his wife. The slight tremor in his voice increased the fear Chad already felt.

It took courage for him to stoop through the doorway. Chad caught his breath when he looked around outside. A magnificent sunrise of gold and orange swept across the sky. The brilliant colors made a

beautiful backdrop. An unusual scene took place before them.

It looked as if there were at least a hundred Papua New Guinean men, women, and children. They stood in clusters of 5 to 10. The clusters formed a line that stretched down the mountain. Smiling faces chanted in Pidgin. One group at a time came toward the flat area in front of Levi's hut.

Chad watched as a family of 5 stepped up to Levi. They added something to a pile at Levi's feet.

"That's cau cau!" Dr. Anderson exclaimed. He jogged up to Dr. Wilson's side. "Cau cau and taro! Food! The whole village is bringing food!"

"Yes!" Levi affirmed, laughing. His eyes shone with joy. "The village leaders came this morning. They said they have watched how God has taken care of my family. They know we did not have any food. Yet we did not starve. They decided that God is more powerful than the evil spirits after all!"

"So they're bringing this food to your family?" Andy asked.

"Yes, and that's not all," Levi answered. "They have asked if we can have a church service this morning. They want to hear about God and His power!"

"Well, praise the Lord!" Dr. Anderson shouted. "Let's go to church!"

The church service was unlike anything Chad had ever experienced. It was held in a building created in hopes of this change of heart. The walls were like the walls of Levi's house. However, they only went halfway to the roof. The top half of the building was open. Only the support poles blocked the view of the mountains and trees.

The opening let a refreshing breeze blow

through. Chad and Andy agreed the open spaces were a good idea. There were so many people in the church that without the breeze the air would become stuffy.

The floor of the building was dirt. The people sat on it or on crude benches made from long strips of wood. Those who couldn't crowd into the building found a place outside, looking in.

"Once this village decides to do something, they really get into it," Andy whispered to Chad.

Levi stood in front of the crowd and preached a powerful message. Many people came to know Christ as their Savior. Some of them testified. One older man in a dusty tweed sports coat strained to get to his feet. Tears poured down his face. He talked in the language of his people. Another man translated into Pidgin. Dr. Anderson translated the Pidgin into English for the Wilsons.

The man spoke in a raspy voice. "We are a people who for generations have had a deep, deep hunger. We have never found anything to satisfy it. But you have come to us, Levi, and started a garden. From this garden, you are giving us food. For the first time, our deep hunger is satisfied.

"You have been faithful to us. Grow the garden. Continue to give us the food that satisfies. Help us grow strong with it."

Chad knew that the man wasn't talking about a vegetable garden. He was speaking of the Word of God. Chad knew what that hunger of the soul felt like. He, too, was experiencing the joy of being satisfied.

After church Chad and his family walked back to Levi's hut. Ruth was already inside. She smiled as they arrived. Cau cau and taro cooked over a roaring fire.

"That man talked about a deep hunger," she said. "My family, too, has known what it is to be hungry. But today the Lord has provided for us! Won't you please join us for lunch?"

"I'm so glad you asked us, Ruth," Dr. Anderson answered. "I wouldn't want to deprive you of this chance to show the Wilsons what a great cook you are! Besides," he continued, "while my spiritual cup is overflowing, none of it has reached my stomach yet!"

Chad's mouth watered as the food cooked. It would be a while before it was ready to eat. He had to get out of the hut until dinner was ready.

It was empty outside. The villagers gathered in their huts. Chad looked at the surrounding jungle. He thought about his adventure the day before. It had been more exciting than any daydream he had ever had. He would never forget what it was like to be lost in the rain forest. But most of all, he would always remember that he was found twice in one day.